I0017340

Google Sheets Essentials

Your Complete Guide to Data Management
and Collaboration

Laine Griffey

All rights reserved. No part of this publication may be reproduced, distributed, or transmitted in any form or by any means, including photocopying, recording, or other electronic or mechanical methods, without the prior written permission of the publisher, except in the case of brief quotations embodied in critical reviews and certain other noncommercial uses permitted by copyright law. For permission requests, write to the publisher at the address below.

Laine Griffey

521 Concord Avenue

Elkhart, Indiana 46516

Introduction to Google Sheets

Purpose of Google Sheets

Google Sheets is a powerful, cloud-based spreadsheet application that enables users to create, edit, and collaborate on spreadsheets in real-time. It offers a wide range of functionalities from basic data entry to advanced data analysis, making it a versatile tool for both personal and professional use. Whether you're managing a budget, analyzing survey results, or preparing a mail merge for a book promotion, Google Sheets provides the tools you need to organize and analyze your data efficiently.

Key Features of Google Sheets

1. **Cloud-Based Accessibility:**
    - Access your spreadsheets from anywhere with an internet connection. All changes are saved automatically in real-time, ensuring that your data is always up-to-date.
2. **Collaboration:**
    - Multiple users can work on the same spreadsheet simultaneously. You can see changes made by others in real-time, leave comments, and chat within the document, enhancing teamwork and productivity.
3. **Integration with Google Workspace:**
    - Google Sheets seamlessly integrates with other Google Workspace apps like Google Docs, Google Slides, Google Forms, and Google Drive. This integration allows for easy data sharing and workflow automation across different tools.

4. **Templates:**
   - Google Sheets offers a variety of templates for common tasks such as budgeting, invoicing, project management, and more. These templates can help you get started quickly and ensure that your spreadsheets are well-organized and professional-looking.
5. **Mobile Compatibility:**
   - The Google Sheets mobile app allows you to view and edit your spreadsheets on the go, providing flexibility and convenience for mobile users.
6. **Data Security:**
   - Google Sheets includes robust security features such as two-factor authentication, encryption, and granular sharing permissions to protect your data.

Overview of Data Analysis Capabilities

Google Sheets comes equipped with numerous features that facilitate data analysis. Users can perform calculations using formulas and functions, visualize data through charts and graphs, and automate tasks with macros. The ability to collaborate with others in real-time also makes it an excellent choice for team projects. Additionally, its integration with other Google Workspace apps and various add-ons extends its functionality beyond a traditional spreadsheet application.

Key Data Analysis Features

1. **Formulas and Functions:**
   - Google Sheets supports a wide range of formulas and functions for performing calculations and data manipulation. These include basic arithmetic functions (SUM, AVERAGE), logical functions (IF, AND, OR), text functions (CONCATENATE, SPLIT), and advanced functions (VLOOKUP, QUERY, ARRAYFORMULA).
2. **Charts and Graphs:**
   - Google Sheets offers a variety of chart types, including column charts, bar charts, line charts, pie charts, scatter plots, and more. These visualizations help you to quickly understand trends, patterns, and outliers in your data.
3. **Pivot Tables:**
   - Pivot tables allow you to summarize and analyze large datasets by organizing and aggregating your data in a flexible and

dynamic manner. You can quickly group, filter, and sort your data to gain insights.

4. **Conditional Formatting:**
   - Conditional formatting helps to highlight important data points or trends by changing the appearance of cells based on specific criteria. This makes it easier to spot patterns and anomalies in your data.

5. **Data Validation:**
   - Data validation rules can be set up to ensure data integrity by restricting the type of data that can be entered into a cell. This helps to maintain consistency and accuracy in your spreadsheets.

6. **Import and Export Data:**
   - Google Sheets allows you to import data from various sources, including CSV files, Excel spreadsheets, and other Google Sheets. You can also export your data to different formats for use in other applications.

7. **Add-ons and Integrations:**
   - Extend the functionality of Google Sheets with add-ons and integrations. Popular add-ons include Supermetrics for marketing data, AutoCrat for document generation, and Google Analytics for web traffic analysis. Integrations with tools like Zapier and IFTTT can automate workflows and connect Google Sheets with other apps.

8. **Scripting and Automation:**
   - Google Apps Script enables you to write custom scripts to automate tasks and enhance the functionality of your

spreadsheets. You can create custom functions, automate repetitive tasks, and integrate with other Google Workspace apps.

Practical Applications

1. **Budget Management:**
   - Track income and expenses, create financial forecasts, and monitor cash flow with customizable budget templates and financial functions.
2. **Project Management:**
   - Plan, track, and manage projects with Gantt charts, task lists, and project timelines. Collaborate with team members in real-time to ensure project success.
3. **Data Collection and Analysis:**
   - Use Google Forms to collect data and automatically import responses into Google Sheets for analysis. Apply statistical functions and create visualizations to interpret survey results.
4. **Sales and Inventory Tracking:**
   - Monitor sales performance, manage inventory levels, and generate sales reports. Use pivot tables and charts to analyze sales trends and forecast future demand.
5. **Mail Merge for Marketing:**
   - Automate personalized email campaigns by merging data from Google Sheets with email templates in Gmail. Track engagement metrics and analyze campaign performance.

6. **Educational Tools:**
    - Teachers can use Google Sheets to track student progress, calculate grades, and analyze assessment data. Collaborative features allow students to work on group projects and assignments.

Formulas and Functions

Basic Formulas

Formulas in Google Sheets perform calculations and return results based on the data in your spreadsheet. Every formula in Google Sheets begins with an equal sign (=).

1. **SUM:**
   - **Description:** Adds all the numbers in a specified range.
   - **Syntax:** `=SUM(range)`
   - **Example:** To add all numbers in cells A2 through A10, you would use:
     `=SUM(A2:A10)`

2. **AVERAGE:**
   - **Description:** Calculates the average (arithmetic mean) of a range of numbers.
   - **Syntax:** `=AVERAGE(range)`
   - **Example:** To find the average of numbers in cells B2 through B10, use:
     `=AVERAGE(B2:B10)`

3. **COUNT:**
   - **Description:** Counts the number of cells in a range that contain numbers.
   - **Syntax:** `=COUNT(range)`
   - **Example:** To count the number of cells with numbers in the range C2 to C10, use:
     `=COUNT(C2:C10)`

4. **COUNTA:**
   - **Description:** Counts the number of cells in a range that are not empty.
   - **Syntax:** `=COUNTA(range)`

- **Example:** To count the number of non-empty cells in the range D2 to D10, use: `=COUNTA(D2:D10)`
5. **MIN and MAX:**
   - **Description:** `MIN` returns the smallest number in a range, while `MAX` returns the largest number.
   - **Syntax:** `=MIN(range)`, `=MAX(range)`
   - **Example:** To find the smallest number in E2 through E10, use: `=MIN(E2:E10)`. For the largest number, use: `=MAX(E2:E10)`

Common Functions for Data Analysis

1. **VLOOKUP:**
   - **Description:** Searches for a value in the first column of a range and returns a value in the same row from a specified column.
   - **Syntax:** `=VLOOKUP(search_key, range, index, [is_sorted])`
   - **Parameters:**
     - `search_key`: The value to search for.
     - `range`: The range of cells to search within.
     - `index`: The column number in the range from which to retrieve the value.
     - `is_sorted`: [Optional] TRUE if the first column is sorted. Defaults to FALSE.
   - **Example:** To find a person's email based on their name, where names are in column A

and emails in column C, use:
```
=VLOOKUP("John Doe", A2:C10, 3,
FALSE)
```

2. **INDEX and MATCH:**
   - **Description:** `INDEX` returns the value of a cell at a specified position in a range, while `MATCH` returns the relative position of a search key in a range.
   - **Syntax:**
     - `INDEX: =INDEX(range, row, [column])`
     - `MATCH: =MATCH(search_key, range, [match_type])`
   - **Parameters:**
     - `range`: The range of cells.
     - `row`: The row number in the range from which to retrieve the value.
     - `column`: [Optional] The column number in the range from which to retrieve the value.
     - `search_key`: The value to search for.
     - `match_type`: [Optional] 1 for less than, 0 for exact match, -1 for greater than.
   - **Example:** To find the email of "John Doe" where names are in column A and emails in column C:
     - `MATCH` to find the row number:
       ```
       =MATCH("John Doe", A2:A10,
       0)
       ```

- INDEX to find the email:
  ```
  =INDEX(C2:C10, MATCH("John
  Doe", A2:A10, 0))
  ```

3. **IF:**
   - **Description:** Returns one value if a condition is true and another value if it's false.
   - **Syntax:** `=IF(condition, value_if_true, value_if_false)`
   - **Parameters:**
     - `condition`: A logical expression that evaluates to TRUE or FALSE.
     - `value_if_true`: The value to return if the condition is true.
     - `value_if_false`: The value to return if the condition is false.
   - **Example:** To label sales amounts in column B as "High" if they are greater than 1000, and "Low" otherwise: `=IF(B2>1000, "High", "Low")`

4. **SUMIF and COUNTIF:**
   - **Description:** SUMIF adds the cells specified by a given condition or criteria, while COUNTIF counts the cells that meet a condition.
   - **Syntax:**
     - SUMIF: `=SUMIF(range, criteria, [sum_range])`
     - COUNTIF: `=COUNTIF(range, criteria)`
   - **Parameters:**

- range: The range of cells to be evaluated by criteria.
      - criteria: The condition to be met.
      - sum_range: [Optional] The actual cells to sum. If omitted, range is summed.
  - **Example:** To sum the sales amounts in column B that are greater than 500: =SUMIF(B2:B10, ">500"). To count the number of sales greater than 500: =COUNTIF(B2:B10, ">500")

5. **CONCATENATE:**
   - **Description:** Joins several text strings into one string.
   - **Syntax:** =CONCATENATE(string1, string2, ...)
   - **Parameters:**
      - string1, string2, ...: The strings to join.
   - **Example:** To join the first name in A2 and the last name in B2 into one full name: =CONCATENATE(A2, " ", B2)

Nested Functions

Combining functions can create powerful formulas to handle more complex tasks.

Example: To create a full name from first and last names in columns A and B and label it "Full Name" only if both fields are not empty:

excel

Copy code

```
=IF(AND(A2<>"", B2<>""), CONCATENATE(A2, "
", B2), "Incomplete Name")
```

Explanation:

- `AND(A2<>"", B2<>"")`: Checks that both A2 and B2 are not empty.
- `CONCATENATE(A2, " ", B2)`: Combines A2 and B2 with a space in between if the condition is met.
- `IF`: Returns "Incomplete Name" if either A2 or B2 is empty.

Data Visualization

Importance of Data Visualization

Data visualization is crucial for interpreting and presenting data in an easily understandable format. Charts and graphs can reveal patterns, trends, and insights that might not be immediately apparent from raw data alone.

Creating Charts and Graphs

Step-by-Step Guide to Inserting a Chart

1. **Select Your Data:**
   - Highlight the range of cells you want to include in the chart. Ensure you include headers to label the data series.
2. **Insert a Chart:**
   - Go to the `Insert` menu and select `Chart`. Alternatively, click the `Chart` icon in the toolbar.
3. **Chart Editor:**
   - The Chart Editor will appear on the right side of the screen, offering various options to customize your chart.

Types of Charts

1. **Column Chart:**
   - **Use Case:** Comparing different categories or groups.
   - **Example:** Comparing monthly sales across different regions.
2. **Bar Chart:**

- Use Case: Similar to column charts but better for long category names.
- Example: Survey responses with long descriptive answers.

3. **Line Chart:**
   - **Use Case:** Displaying trends over time.
   - **Example:** Tracking website traffic over several months.

4. **Pie Chart:**
   - **Use Case:** Showing proportions of a whole.
   - **Example:** Market share of different companies.

5. **Scatter Plot:**
   - **Use Case:** Identifying correlations between two variables.
   - **Example:** Relationship between advertising spend and sales revenue.

6. **Area Chart:**
   - **Use Case:** Showing cumulative totals over time.
   - **Example:** Cumulative rainfall over a year.

Customizing Charts

1. **Chart Title and Labels:**
   - Click on the chart title to edit it.
   - Use the Chart Editor to add and customize axis titles.

2. **Chart Type:**
   - In the Chart Editor, under the Setup tab, you can change the chart type to better fit your data.

3. **Data Range:**

- Adjust the data range if needed by clicking on the range selector in the Chart Editor.

4. **Series Customization:**
   - Customize individual data series by clicking on the series name in the Chart Editor. You can change colors, line styles, and point shapes.

5. **Axis Customization:**
   - Under the `Customize` tab, you can format the vertical and horizontal axes. Options include adjusting scales, adding gridlines, and setting minimum and maximum values.

6. **Legend:**
   - Adjust the legend's position and format under the `Customize` tab. You can place it at the top, bottom, left, right, or inside the chart.

Practical Example

Example: Monthly Sales Analysis

1. **Data Preparation:**
   - Suppose you have monthly sales data for different regions in a sheet with headers: "Month," "Region A," "Region B," and "Region C."

2. **Selecting Data:**
   - Highlight the data range including headers: `A1:D13`.

3. **Inserting the Chart:**
   - Go to `Insert` > `Chart` and select `Column chart` in the Chart Editor.

4. **Customizing the Chart:**

- **Chart Title:** Change the title to "Monthly Sales Analysis."
- **Axis Titles:** Add "Month" as the horizontal axis title and "Sales" as the vertical axis title.
- **Series Colors:** Customize each region's color for clarity.
5. **Advanced Customization:**
   - **Annotations:** Add annotations to highlight significant data points.
   - **Trendlines:** Add trendlines to each series to show overall trends.

Using Conditional Formatting for Visual Data Analysis

1. **Highlighting Important Data:**
   - Use conditional formatting to highlight cells based on specific criteria. For example, highlight sales above a certain threshold.
2. **Applying Conditional Formatting:**
   - Select the range you want to format.
   - Go to Format > Conditional formatting.
   - Set the criteria (e.g., Greater than a specific value) and choose a formatting style.

Creating Dynamic Charts with Filtered Data

1. **Adding a Filter:**
   - Click the Data menu and select Create a filter.

2. **Filtering Data:**
    o Use the filter dropdowns in the header row to filter data dynamically. This updates the chart in real-time based on the selected criteria.

Interactive Dashboards

Google Sheets allows you to create interactive dashboards that combine multiple charts and tables.

1. **Linking Charts and Data:**
    o Combine various charts and data tables on a single sheet to create a dashboard.
    o Use slicers (from the `Data` menu) to add interactive controls to filter data across multiple charts simultaneously.
2. **Embedding Charts:**
    o You can embed charts from Google Sheets into Google Docs or Google Slides, keeping them updated automatically when the data changes.

Exporting and Sharing Charts

1. **Exporting Charts:**
    o Right-click on the chart and select `Download`. Choose the desired format (e.g., PNG, PDF, SVG).
2. **Sharing Charts:**
    o Charts embedded in a shared Google Sheet will be visible to collaborators with the appropriate permissions.

- ○ You can also publish charts to the web by selecting `File` > `Publish to the web`.

Advanced Features

Using Pivot Tables

Pivot tables are powerful tools for summarizing, analyzing, and exploring large datasets. They allow you to reorganize and aggregate data without altering the original data.

Creating a Pivot Table

1. **Select Your Data:**
   - Highlight the range of cells that contain the data you want to analyze. Ensure your data includes headers.
2. **Insert a Pivot Table:**
   - Go to the `Data` menu and select `Pivot table`.
   - In the pop-up window, choose whether to create the pivot table in a new sheet or in the existing sheet.
3. **Configure the Pivot Table:**
   - The Pivot Table Editor will appear on the right side of the screen. You can now set up rows, columns, values, and filters.

Example: Sales Data Analysis

Suppose you have sales data with columns for Date, Region, Product, and Sales Amount.

1. **Rows:**
   - Add the `Region` field to the Rows section to list sales by region.
2. **Values:**

- Add the `Sales Amount` field to the Values section to sum the sales amounts for each region.
3. **Columns:**
   - Add the `Product` field to the Columns section to see sales distribution by product for each region.
4. **Filters:**
   - Add the `Date` field to the Filters section to analyze sales for a specific date range.

Importing Data from External Sources

Google Sheets allows you to import data from various external sources, such as other spreadsheets, CSV files, and online databases.

Importing Data from a CSV File

1. **Open the Import Menu:**
   - Click the `File` menu and select `Import`.
2. **Select the File:**
   - Choose the `Upload` tab, then drag and drop your CSV file or select it from your computer.
3. **Configure Import Options:**
   - Choose how to import the data (e.g., create a new sheet, insert new rows, or replace data at selected cell).
   - Click `Import data`.

Importing Data from Another Google Sheet

1. **Use the `IMPORTRANGE` Function:**

- Syntax:
  ```
  =IMPORTRANGE(spreadsheet_url,
  range_string)
  ```
- **Example:** To import data from a sheet with URL
  ```
  https://docs.google.com/spreadsh
  eets/d/abc123
  ```
  and range
  ```
  Sheet1!A1:D10
  ```
  , use:
  ```
  =IMPORTRANGE("https://docs.googl
  e.com/spreadsheets/d/abc123",
  "Sheet1!A1:D10")
  ```

2. **Grant Access:**
   - The first time you use `IMPORTRANGE` with a new source spreadsheet, you'll need to grant access.

Using Add-ons and Integrations

Google Sheets supports a variety of add-ons that extend its functionality. Add-ons can automate tasks, integrate with other services, and provide advanced features not built into Google Sheets.

Installing Add-ons

1. **Open the Add-ons Menu:**
   - Click the `Extensions` menu, then choose `Add-ons` and `Get add-ons`.
2. **Browse and Install:**
   - Browse the available add-ons or search for specific ones. Click on an add-on to see details and install it.

Popular Add-ons

1. **Supermetrics:**
   - **Use Case:** Import data from marketing platforms (e.g., Google Analytics, Facebook Ads) directly into Google Sheets.
   - **Installation:** Search for Supermetrics in the Add-ons store and follow the prompts to install.
2. **AutoCrat:**
   - **Use Case:** Automate document and report generation from data in Google Sheets.
   - **Installation:** Search for AutoCrat in the Add-ons store and follow the prompts to install.
3. **Mail Merge with Attachments:**
   - **Use Case:** Send personalized emails with attachments using data from Google Sheets.
   - **Installation:** Search for Mail Merge with Attachments in the Add-ons store and follow the prompts to install.

Advanced Formulas and Functions

1. **ARRAYFORMULA:**
   - **Description:** Applies a function to a range of cells.
   - **Syntax:**
     ```
     =ARRAYFORMULA(function(range))
     ```
   - **Example:** To multiply all values in column A by 2, use: `=ARRAYFORMULA(A2:A10 * 2)`
2. **QUERY:**

- Description: Runs a query on a data range using SQL-like syntax.
- Syntax: `=QUERY(data, query, [headers])`
- Example: To select rows where the sales amount in column B is greater than 500, use: `=QUERY(A1:B10, "SELECT * WHERE B > 500")`

3. **SPARKLINE:**
   - Description: Creates a miniature chart within a single cell.
   - Syntax: `=SPARKLINE(data, [options])`
   - Example: To create a sparkline for data in cells A2 to A10, use: `=SPARKLINE(A2:A10)`
   - Options: Customize the sparkline type, color, and other attributes.

Using Google Apps Script

Google Apps Script allows you to write custom scripts to automate tasks and enhance Google Sheets functionality.

1. **Access Google Apps Script:**
   - Go to `Extensions` > `Apps Script`.
2. **Write a Script:**

Use JavaScript to write your custom script. For example, a script to automatically sort data might look like this:
javascript
Copy code

```
function sortData() {
```

```
  var sheet =
SpreadsheetApp.getActiveSpreadsheet().getAc
tiveSheet();

  var range = sheet.getRange("A2:B10");

  range.sort({column: 1, ascending: true});

}
```

  o

3. **Run the Script:**
    o Save your script and run it from the Apps
      Script editor. You can also set up triggers to
      run the script automatically.

Practical Example: Creating a Dynamic Dashboard

1. **Data Setup:**
    o Prepare your data in a structured format
      with headers.
2. **Create Pivot Tables and Charts:**
    o Insert pivot tables and charts to summarize
      and visualize key metrics.
3. **Add Slicers:**
    o Use slicers to create interactive filters that
      update multiple charts and tables
      simultaneously.
    o To add a slicer, click the Data menu, then
      select Slicer. Configure the slicer to filter
      data based on specific criteria.
4. **Design the Dashboard:**

- Arrange the pivot tables, charts, and slicers on a single sheet to create a cohesive dashboard.
- Use cell formatting and borders to enhance the visual appeal and organization of the dashboard.

Exporting and Sharing Data

1. **Exporting Data:**
   - Go to the `File` menu and select `Download` to export the data in various formats (e.g., Excel, PDF, CSV).
2. **Publishing to the Web:**
   - To share your spreadsheet online, go to the `File` menu and select `Publish to the web`. Choose the format and specific sheets or ranges you want to publish.
   - You can embed the published content in a website or share the link with others.
3. **Sharing and Collaboration:**
   - Click the `Share` button to invite collaborators and set their permissions (Viewer, Commenter, Editor).

Collaborating and Sharing

Introduction

Google Sheets offers powerful collaboration features that allow multiple users to work on a single spreadsheet simultaneously. This section will guide you through the various collaboration and sharing options available in

Google Sheets, including setting permissions, adding comments, tracking changes, and more.

Sharing Sheets with Others

Step-by-Step Guide to Sharing a Sheet

1. **Open the Spreadsheet:**
   - Ensure your spreadsheet is saved in Google Drive.
2. **Click the Share Button:**
   - In the top-right corner of the screen, click the blue `Share` button.
3. **Add People:**
   - In the sharing settings window, enter the email addresses of the people you want to share the sheet with.
   - You can also generate a shareable link by clicking `Get shareable link`.
4. **Set Permissions:**
   - Choose the permission level for each person:
     - **Viewer:** Can view but not make any changes.
     - **Commenter:** Can view and add comments but not edit the content.
     - **Editor:** Can view, comment, and make changes to the content.
5. **Send Invitations:**
   - After setting permissions, click `Send` to notify the users via email.

Sharing Settings and Permissions

1. **Changing Permissions:**
   - To change permissions after sharing, click Share again, then click on the pencil icon next to a person's name to adjust their access level.
2. **Remove Access:**
   - To remove someone's access, click the X next to their name in the sharing settings window.
3. **Advanced Sharing Settings:**
   - Click on Advanced in the sharing settings window to see more options, such as preventing editors from changing access and adding new people or disabling options to download, print, and copy for commenters and viewers.

Adding Comments and Notes

1. **Adding Comments:**
   - Select the cell you want to comment on.
   - Go to the Insert menu and select Comment, or right-click the cell and choose Comment.
   - Type your comment in the box that appears and click Comment.
2. **Replying to Comments:**
   - Click on a comment to expand it, then type your reply in the reply box and click Reply.
3. **Resolving Comments:**
   - Once a comment has been addressed, click the Resolve button to mark it as resolved. Resolved comments are hidden but can be

viewed by clicking `Comments` in the top-right corner and selecting `See all comments`.

4. **Adding Notes:**
   - Notes are useful for adding additional context without needing a full comment thread.
   - Select the cell, go to the `Insert` menu, and select `Note`.

Viewing and Tracking Changes

1. **Version History:**
   - Google Sheets automatically saves versions of your document. To view the version history, go to the `File` menu and select `Version history`, then `See version history`.
   - You can view previous versions, see who made changes, and restore any version if necessary.
2. **Named Versions:**
   - To name a specific version, open the version history, click the three dots next to a version, and select `Name this version`.
3. **Show Edits:**
   - To see recent edits, click `Last edit was...` at the top of the screen. This shows the most recent changes and who made them.

Chatting in Real-Time

1. **In-Sheet Chat:**
   - If multiple users are working on the spreadsheet at the same time, a chat icon will appear in the top-right corner. Click the icon to open a chat window and communicate in real-time.

Using Notifications

1. **Set Up Notifications:**
   - To receive email notifications about changes, go to the `Tools` menu and select `Notification rules`.
   - Choose the criteria for notifications (e.g., when any changes are made, when a user submits a form) and click `Save`.

Publishing Sheets

1. **Publishing to the Web:**
   - Go to the `File` menu and select `Publish to the web`.
   - Choose whether to publish the entire document or specific sheets/ranges.
   - Click `Publish`, then share the link provided or embed it in a website.

Embedding Sheets in Google Docs and Slides

1. **Embedding a Chart:**
   - Select the chart in Google Sheets.

- ○ Go to the `Edit` menu, click `Copy`, then open the Google Doc or Slide where you want to embed it.
- ○ Go to the `Edit` menu in the Google Doc/Slide, click `Paste`, and choose to link the chart to the spreadsheet.

2. **Embedding a Range:**
   - ○ Select the range of cells you want to embed.
   - ○ Copy the selected range, then paste it into the Google Doc or Slide. When pasting, choose the option to link to the spreadsheet to keep the data synced.

Using Google Drive for File Management

1. **Organizing Files:**
   - ○ Create folders in Google Drive to organize your spreadsheets. Drag and drop sheets into the appropriate folders.
2. **Shared Drives:**
   - ○ Use Shared Drives for team projects. Files in Shared Drives are owned by the team rather than individuals, ensuring continued access if a team member leaves.

Advanced Collaboration Tools

1. **Google Workspace Integration:**
   - ○ Utilize Google Workspace (formerly G Suite) apps for seamless collaboration across Gmail, Calendar, Drive, Docs, Sheets, Slides, and Meet.
2. **Using Google Meet:**

- Start a Google Meet session directly from Google Sheets by clicking the camera icon in the top-right corner, allowing real-time video collaboration.
3. **Project Management:**
   - Integrate project management tools like Asana or Trello with Google Sheets to streamline task tracking and project updates.

Advanced Features

Using Pivot Tables

Pivot tables are essential for summarizing, analyzing, and exploring large datasets. They allow you to reorganize and aggregate data dynamically.

Creating a Pivot Table

1. **Select Your Data:**
    - Highlight the range of cells that contain the data you want to analyze. Ensure your data includes headers.
2. **Insert a Pivot Table:**
    - Go to the `Data` menu and select `Pivot table`.
    - Choose whether to create the pivot table in a new sheet or in the existing sheet.
3. **Configure the Pivot Table:**
    - The Pivot Table Editor will appear on the right side. Set up rows, columns, values, and filters.

Example: Sales Data Analysis

Suppose you have sales data with columns for Date, Region, Product, and Sales Amount.

1. **Rows:**
    - Add the `Region` field to the Rows section to list sales by region.
2. **Values:**

- Add the `Sales Amount` field to the Values section to sum the sales amounts for each region.

3. **Columns:**
   - Add the `Product` field to the Columns section to see sales distribution by product for each region.

4. **Filters:**
   - Add the `Date` field to the Filters section to analyze sales for a specific date range.

Importing Data from External Sources

Google Sheets allows you to import data from various external sources, such as other spreadsheets, CSV files, and online databases.

Importing Data from a CSV File

1. **Open the Import Menu:**
   - Click the `File` menu and select `Import`.

2. **Select the File:**
   - Choose the `Upload` tab, then drag and drop your CSV file or select it from your computer.

3. **Configure Import Options:**
   - Choose how to import the data (e.g., create a new sheet, insert new rows, or replace data at selected cell).
   - Click `Import data`.

Importing Data from Another Google Sheet

1. **Use the `IMPORTRANGE` Function:**

- Syntax:
  ```
  =IMPORTRANGE(spreadsheet_url,
  range_string)
  ```
- **Example:** To import data from a sheet with URL
  ```
  https://docs.google.com/spreadsh
  eets/d/abc123
  ```
  and range `Sheet1!A1:D10`, use:
  ```
  =IMPORTRANGE("https://docs.googl
  e.com/spreadsheets/d/abc123",
  "Sheet1!A1:D10")
  ```

2. **Grant Access:**
   - The first time you use `IMPORTRANGE` with a new source spreadsheet, you'll need to grant access.

Importing Data from Online Sources

1. **Use the `IMPORTDATA` Function:**
   - **Syntax:** `=IMPORTDATA(url)`
   - **Example:** To import data from a public CSV file, use:
     ```
     =IMPORTDATA("https://example.com
     /data.csv")
     ```

2. **Use the `IMPORTHTML` Function:**
   - **Syntax:** `=IMPORTHTML(url, query, index)`
   - **Parameters:**
     - `url`: The URL of the web page.
     - `query`: The type of data to import (`table` or `list`).

- - `index`: The index of the table or list on the web page.
  - **Example:** To import the first table from a webpage, use:
    ```
    =IMPORTHTML("https://example.com
    /page", "table", 1)
    ```

Using Add-ons and Integrations

Google Sheets supports a variety of add-ons that extend its functionality. Add-ons can automate tasks, integrate with other services, and provide advanced features not built into Google Sheets.

Installing Add-ons

1. **Open the Add-ons Menu:**
   - Click the `Extensions` menu, then choose `Add-ons` and `Get add-ons`.
2. **Browse and Install:**
   - Browse the available add-ons or search for specific ones. Click on an add-on to see details and install it.

Popular Add-ons

1. **Supermetrics:**
   - **Use Case:** Import data from marketing platforms (e.g., Google Analytics, Facebook Ads) directly into Google Sheets.
   - **Installation:** Search for Supermetrics in the Add-ons store and follow the prompts to install.
2. **AutoCrat:**

- Use Case: Automate document and report generation from data in Google Sheets.
- Installation: Search for AutoCrat in the Add-ons store and follow the prompts to install.

3. **Mail Merge with Attachments:**
   - **Use Case:** Send personalized emails with attachments using data from Google Sheets.
   - **Installation:** Search for Mail Merge with Attachments in the Add-ons store and follow the prompts to install.

Advanced Formulas and Functions

1. **ARRAYFORMULA:**
   - **Description:** Applies a function to a range of cells.
   - **Syntax:**
     `=ARRAYFORMULA(function(range))`
   - **Example:** To multiply all values in column A by 2, use: `=ARRAYFORMULA(A2:A10 * 2)`

2. **QUERY:**
   - **Description:** Runs a query on a data range using SQL-like syntax.
   - **Syntax:** `=QUERY(data, query, [headers])`
   - **Example:** To select rows where the sales amount in column B is greater than 500, use: `=QUERY(A1:B10, "SELECT * WHERE B > 500")`

3. **SPARKLINE:**

- **Description:** Creates a miniature chart within a single cell.
- **Syntax:** `=SPARKLINE(data, [options])`
- **Example:** To create a sparkline for data in cells A2 to A10, use: `=SPARKLINE(A2:A10)`
- **Options:** Customize the sparkline type, color, and other attributes.

4. **GOOGLEFINANCE:**
   - **Description:** Fetches current or historical securities information from Google Finance.
   - **Syntax:** `=GOOGLEFINANCE(ticker, [attribute], [start_date], [end_date], [interval])`
   - **Example:** To get the current price of Google stock, use: `=GOOGLEFINANCE("GOOG")`

Using Google Apps Script

Google Apps Script allows you to write custom scripts to automate tasks and enhance Google Sheets functionality.

1. **Access Google Apps Script:**
   - Go to `Extensions > Apps Script`.
2. **Write a Script:**

Use JavaScript to write your custom script. For example, a script to automatically sort data might look like this:
javascript
Copy code

```
function sortData() {
```

```
    var sheet =
SpreadsheetApp.getActiveSpreadsheet().getAc
tiveSheet();

    var range = sheet.getRange("A2:B10");

    range.sort({column: 1, ascending: true});

}
```

    o

  3. **Run the Script:**
    o Save your script and run it from the Apps
     Script editor. You can also set up triggers to
     run the script automatically.

Example: Automating Data Entry

Suppose you want to automate the process of adding a
timestamp whenever new data is entered.

Write the Script:
javascript
Copy code

```
function onEdit(e) {

    var sheet = e.source.getActiveSheet();

    var range = e.range;

    if (range.getColumn() == 1 &&
range.getRow() > 1 && range.getValue() !==
"") {
```

```
  var date = new Date();

  sheet.getRange(range.getRow(),
2).setValue(date);

  }

}
```

1.
2. **Set Up the Trigger:**
   ○ In the Apps Script editor, go to `Triggers` (clock icon), then click `Add Trigger`.
   ○ Set the function to `onEdit`, the event type to `On edit`, and save.

Practical Example: Creating a Dynamic Dashboard

1. **Data Setup:**
   ○ Prepare your data in a structured format with headers.
2. **Create Pivot Tables and Charts:**
   ○ Insert pivot tables and charts to summarize and visualize key metrics.
3. **Add Slicers:**
   ○ Use slicers to create interactive filters that update multiple charts and tables simultaneously.
   ○ To add a slicer, click the `Data` menu, then select `Slicer`. Configure the slicer to filter data based on specific criteria.
4. **Design the Dashboard:**

- Arrange the pivot tables, charts, and slicers on a single sheet to create a cohesive dashboard.
- Use cell formatting and borders to enhance the visual appeal and organization of the dashboard.

Exporting and Sharing Data

1. **Exporting Data:**
   - Go to the `File` menu and select `Download` to export the data in various formats (e.g., Excel, PDF, CSV).
2. **Publishing to the Web:**
   - To share your spreadsheet online, go to the `File` menu and select `Publish to the web`. Choose the format and specific sheets or ranges you want to publish.
   - You can embed the published content in a website or share the link with others.
3. **Sharing and Collaboration:**
   - Click the `Share` button to invite collaborators and set their permissions (Viewer, Commenter, Editor).

Practical Example: Creating a Dynamic Dashboard

Step 1: Data Setup

1. **Prepare Your Data:**

- Ensure your data is structured in a tabular format with headers. For this example, let's assume you have sales data with the following columns:
  - Date
  - Region
  - Product
  - Sales Amount

2. **Input Your Data:**
   - Enter the data into a Google Sheet. Your data might look something like this:

Date	Region	Product	Sales Amount
2024-01-01	North	A	1000
2024-01-01	South	B	1500
2024-01-02	North	A	1200
2024-01-02	East	C	800
...	...	...	...

Step 2: Create Pivot Tables and Charts

1. **Insert a Pivot Table:**
   - Select the range of your data, including headers.
   - Go to the `Data` menu and select `Pivot table`.
   - Choose to place the pivot table in a new sheet.
2. **Configure the Pivot Table:**
   - In the Pivot Table Editor, add `Region` to the Rows section.
   - Add `Sales Amount` to the Values section and set it to `SUM`.
   - Optionally, add `Date` to the Filters section to allow date-based filtering.
3. **Insert a Chart:**
   - Select the pivot table data.
   - Go to the `Insert` menu and select `Chart`.
   - Choose a suitable chart type, such as a column chart, to visualize the sales by region.

Step 3: Add Slicers

1. **Insert Slicers:**
   - Go to the `Data` menu and select `Slicer`.
   - Place the slicer on the same sheet as your pivot table and chart.
   - Configure the slicer to filter by `Region` or `Date`.
2. **Use the Slicer:**

- Click on the slicer and select the desired region or date range. The pivot table and chart will update automatically to reflect the selected data.

Step 4: Design the Dashboard

1. **Organize Your Dashboard:**
   - Arrange your pivot tables, charts, and slicers in a visually appealing layout.
   - Ensure that your dashboard is easy to read and interpret.
2. **Format Your Dashboard:**
   - Use cell formatting, borders, and colors to enhance the visual appeal.
   - Add titles and labels to your charts and tables for clarity.

Example Layout

Let's assume your dashboard layout looks something like this:

1. **Top Section: Filters**
   - Place slicers at the top for `Region` and `Date`.
2. **Middle Section: Summary Metrics**
   - Place pivot tables summarizing key metrics, such as total sales by region.
3. **Bottom Section: Visualizations**
   - Include various charts, such as a line chart showing sales trends over time, a bar chart for sales by product, and a pie chart for sales distribution by region.

Screenshot Examples (Illustrative)

1. **Slicers at the Top:**
2. **Pivot Table Summarizing Sales:**
3. **Charts Visualizing Sales Data:**

Step 5: Adding Interactive Elements

1. **Use Dropdowns:**
   - Insert dropdowns to allow users to select specific data points. For example, use data validation to create a dropdown list of products.
2. **Create Dynamic Text:**
   - Use formulas like TEXTJOIN or ARRAYFORMULA to create dynamic text elements that update based on selected data.
3. **Link to Detailed Reports:**
   - Add hyperlinks to specific cells or charts that open detailed reports or additional sheets with more granular data.

Step 6: Sharing and Collaboration

1. **Share the Dashboard:**
   - Click the Share button in the top-right corner.
   - Enter the email addresses of collaborators and set their permissions (Viewer, Commenter, Editor).
2. **Enable Notifications:**
   - Set up notifications for changes by going to Tools > Notification rules.

3. **Publish to the Web:**
    - To make your dashboard publicly accessible, go to `File` > `Publish to the web`. Select the sheets or ranges you want to publish and share the link.

Step 7: Automating with Google Apps Script

1. **Write a Script to Refresh Data:**
    - Open the Apps Script editor from `Extensions` > `Apps Script`.

Write a script to refresh the data at regular intervals, such as every hour.
javascript
Copy code

```javascript
function refreshData() {

  var sheet =
SpreadsheetApp.getActiveSpreadsheet().getSh
eetByName("SalesData");

  sheet.getRange("A1").setValue(new
Date()); // Dummy action to trigger refresh

}
```

    -

2. **Set Up a Trigger:**
    - In the Apps Script editor, go to `Triggers` (clock icon), and create a new trigger.
    - Set it to run the `refreshData` function every hour.

www.ingramcontent.com/pod-product-compliance
Lightning Source LLC
LaVergne TN
LVHW051622050326
832903LV00033B/4619

* 9 7 9 8 3 3 4 8 4 2 9 9 1 *